THE STANDARD RESPONSE PROTOCOL

K12

Operational Guidance for Implementing The Standard Response Protocol In a K12 Environment

K12 SCHOOLS AND DISTRICTS

HOLD　　**SECURE**　　**LOCKDOWN**　　**EVACUATE**　　**SHELTER**

i love u guys
FOUNDATION®

PEACE

It does not mean to be in a place where there is no noise, trouble, or hard work.

It means to be in the midst of those things and still be calm in your heart.

STANDARD RESPONSE PROTOCOL

SRP K12 2021 CHANGE HISTORY

AUTHOR/CONTRIBUTOR	VERSION	REVISION DATE	REVISION COMMENTARY
John-Michael Keyes	1.0	03/02/2009	Original content
Russ Deffner John-Michael Keyes	2.0	01/08/2015	Version update. See: The Standard Response Protocol V2 An Overview of What's New in the SRP
Tom Kelley (TxSSC)	2.1	12/02/2017	Content, edits, formal inclusion of the Standard Response Protocol Extended "Hold in your classroom". Texas School Safety Center version
John-Michael Keyes	2.2	05/22/2018	Content, edits. Colorado School District Self Insurance Pool version.
John-Michael Keyes	3.0	06/05/2019	Incorporated "Hold in your classroom or area" into the Standard Response Protocol
John-Michael Keyes	4.0	01/17/2020	Replaced Term of Art Lockout with Secure
Ellen Stoddard-Keyes	4.0	06/23/2020	Added Communications section. Incorporated Review Committee suggestions.

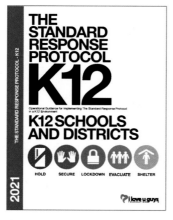

A General Guide on Incorporating the Standard Response Protocol within a School Safety Plan - K-12

Version 4.0
ISBN-13: 978-1-951260-00-2

AUTHOR/CONTRIBUTOR INFORMATION

John-Michael Keyes - Primary Author
Executive Director, The "I Love U Guys" Foundation
johnmichael@iloveuguys.org

Russell Deffner - Contributing Author
The "I Love U Guys" Foundation
Advisor/Contractor/Volunteer

Tom Kelley - Contributor, Texas School Safety Center

Lee Shaughnessy - Reviewer
The "I Love U Guys" Foundation Volunteer

Dr. David Benke - Teacher Guidance
The "I Love U Guys" Foundation Board of Directors
david@iloveuguys.org

Janet Redford - Reviewer
The "I Love U Guys" Foundation Volunteer

SRP REVIEW COMMITTEE

The "I Love U Guys" Foundation SRP Review Committee is comprised of safety stakeholders from a variety of perspectives and professions. The charter of the committee is to advise on the merits of any substantive changes to The Standard Response Protocol. This ensures that changes will not be incorporated into the SRP without consideration or deliberation.

The SRP Review Committee communicates on substantive changes to the SRP primarily through the electronic means of email or teleconference.

The following are the current members of the SRP Review Committee.

Heilit Biehl, Threat Assessment Coordinator, Adams 12 Five Star Schools, Colorado

Kevin Burd, Detective Lieutenant (Ret.), Priority of Life Training and Consulting, Hampton, NJ

Kevin Carroll, Executive Director, JeffCo DeAngelis Foundation, Colorado

Melissa Craven, Director of Emergency Management, Department of Safety, Denver Public Schools, Colorado

Kristen Devitt, M.Ed., CTM, Director, State of Wisconsin Department of Justice, Office of School Safety

Ian Lopez, Director of Safety & Security, Cherry Creek Schools, Colorado

Glenn Rehberg, Deputy Director, State of Wisconsin Department of Justice, Office of School Safety

Jaclyn Schildkraut, PhD, Associate Professor, Department of Criminal Justice, State University of New York at Oswego

Brad Stiles, M.A., Emergency Response Outreach Consultant, Colorado School Safety Resource Center

Mike Thompson, Assistant Director of School Security, Syracuse City School District, New York

SPECIAL THANKS

Joleen Reefe - City and County of Broomfield (Joleen coined the phrase, "Locks, Lights, Out of Sight.")

Pat Hamilton – Chief Operating Officer, Adams 12 Five Star Schools, Colorado

John McDonald – Executive Director, Safety, Security and Emergency Planning, Jefferson County Public Schools, Colorado

Heidi Walts – Commander, Northglenn Police Department, Colorado

Marta Alejandro – Spanish teacher and bilingual educational support professional / Spanish translator and interpreter

CONTACT INFORMATION

The "I Love U Guys" Foundation can be reached online at http://iloveuguys.org.

Email: srp@iloveuguys.org.

The "I Love U Guys" Foundation
PO Box 919
Conifer, CO 80433
303.426.3100

REQUEST FOR COMMENT

The Standard Response Protocol is a synthesis of common practices in use at a number of districts, departments and agencies. The evolution of SRP has included review, comment and suggestion from a number of practitioners. As of 2020, the SRP has been subjected to tactical scrutiny by hundreds of law enforcement agencies and operational review and adoption by thousands of schools.

Suggestions for modification can be made via email at srp_rfc@iloveuguys.org. Please include contact information, district, department or agency, including day time phone.

WARNINGS AND DISCLAIMER

Every effort has been made to make this book as complete and accurate as possible, but no warranty or fitness is implied. The information provided is on an "as is" basis. Please visit our website (https://iloveuguys.org) for the detailed information.

"Tactics are intel driven."

What we plan is based on what we know.

"But the environment dictates tactics."

But what we do, is based on where we are.

– Deputy Chief A.J. DeAndrea
– Civilian Translation: John-Michael Keyes

TABLE OF CONTENTS

STANDARD RESPONSE PROTOCOL

THE "I LOVE U GUYS" FOUNDATION
On September 27th, 2006 a gunman entered Platte Canyon High School in Bailey, Colorado, held seven girls hostage and ultimately shot and killed Emily Keyes. During the time she was held hostage, Emily sent her parents text messages... "I love you guys" and "I love u guys. k?"

Emily's kindness, spirit, fierce joy, and the dignity and grace that followed this tragic event define the core of The "I Love U Guys" Foundation.

MISSION
The "I Love U Guys" Foundation was created to restore and protect the joy of youth through educational programs and positive actions in collaboration with families, schools, communities, organizations and government entities.

COMMITMENT
There are several things we are committed to. The most important thing we can do is offer our material at no cost to schools, districts, departments, agencies and organizations. The reason we are able to continue to provide this service is due, in part, to the generosity of our donors and Mission Partners (see Partner with Love on the website). The "I Love U Guys" Foundation works very hard to keep our costs down as well as any costs associated with our printed materials. Donor and Mission Partner support allows us to stretch those dollars and services even more. Your gift, no matter the size, helps us achieve our mission. Your help makes a difference to the students, teachers, first responders, and the communities in which we live and work.

ABOUT THIS BOOK
Since 2015, The Foundation offered optional classroom training that included "Hold in your classroom." In 2017, The Foundation developed materials for The Standard Response Protocol Extended (SRP-X) that included the Hold action.

For SRP 2021, the Hold action is incorporated into the Standard Response Protocol.

Also for SRP 2021, the Lockout action is being changed to Secure.

As you begin to implement and drill the protocol, keep in mind that environments are different. What that means is that we provide you with some tactics. Things we know. But your school, your agencies, and your environment, will ultimately dictate what you do.

Please, in your planning, if you see something here that doesn't seem to work in your environment, figure out what does. Let us know.

COPYRIGHTS AND TRADEMARKS
In order to protect the integrity and consistency of The Standard Response Protocol, The "I Love U Guys" Foundation exercises all protection under copyright and trademark. Use of this material is governed by the Terms of Use or a Commercial Licensing Agreement.

COMMERCIAL LICENSING
Incorporating the SRP into a commercial product, like software or publication, requires a commercial license. Please contact The "I Love U Guys" Foundation for more information and costs.

TERMS OF USE
Schools, districts, departments, agencies and organizations may use these materials, at no cost, under the following conditions:

1. Materials are not re-sold
2. Core actions and directives are not modified
    2.1. Hold - "In Your Room or Area. Clear the Halls"
    2.2. Secure -"Get Inside, Lock Outside Doors"
    2.3. Lockdown - "Locks, Lights, Out of Sight"
    2.4. Evacuate - A Location may be specified
    2.5. Shelter - followed by the Hazard and the Safety Strategy
3. The Notification of Intent (NOI) is used when the materials are being evaluated. A sample NOI can be downloaded from the website, and is provided to The "I Love U Guys" Foundation through one of the following:
    3.1. Complete the NOI and email it to srp@iloveuguys.org
    3.2. Send an email to srp@iloveuguys.org
4. The Memorandum of Understating (MOU) is used when it has been determined that the materials will be used. A sample MOU can be downloaded from the website, and is provided to The "I Love U Guys" Foundation by emailing it to srp@iloveuguys.org
5. The following modifications to the materials (Handouts, cards) are allowable:
    5.1. Localization of evacuation events
    5.2. Localization of shelter events
    5.3. Addition of organization logo

STANDARD RESPONSE PROTOCOL

CERTIFICATION PROGRAMS

The "I Love U Guys" Foundation is committed to providing its programs at no cost to a widening variety of organizations.

To assess the fidelity of implementation within an organization, the Foundation has developed a certification program for the Standard Response Protocol. The certification program is optional and is not required to use the SRP within your organization.

THE "I LOVE U GUYS" FOUNDATION MOUs OR NOTICE OF INTENT

Some schools, districts, departments and agencies may also desire a formalized Memorandum of Understanding (MOU) with The "I Love U Guys" Foundation. Please visit https://iloveuguys.org for a current version of the MOU. The purpose of this MOU is to define responsibilities of each party and provide scope, clarity of expectations. It affirms agreement of stated protocol by schools, districts, departments and agencies. It also confirms the online availability of the Foundation's materials.

An additional benefit for the Foundation is in seeking funding. Some private grantors view the MOU as a demonstration of program effectiveness.

Another option is to formally notify the Foundation with a Notice of Intent (NOI). This is a notice that you are reviewing the materials but have not adopted them yet. This is also available on the website.

At a minimum, schools, districts, departments and agencies that will ultimately incorporate the SRP into their safety plans and practices should email srp@iloveuguys.org and let us know.

PRIVACY POLICY

When you agree to the Terms of Use by sending an MOU or NOI, your contact information will be entered into a database. You will receive notification when there are updates and/or new materials. You will have the opportunity to opt in to receive periodic blog posts and newsletters via email.

Our Commitment to Program Users: We will not sell, share or trade names, contact, or personal information with any other entity, nor send mailings to our donors on behalf of other organizations.

This policy applies to all information received by The "I Love U Guys" Foundation, both online and offline, as well as any electronic, written, or oral communications.

Please see our website for the full Privacy text.

ONE DEMAND

The protocol also carries an obligation. Kids and teens are smart. An implicit part of the SRP is that authorities and school personnel tell students what's going on.

Certainly, temper it at the elementary school level, but middle schoolers and older need accurate information for the greatest survivability, and to minimize panic and assist recovery.

Note: Student training includes preparation for some alternative methods during a tactical response but reinforces deference to local law enforcement.

STANDARD RESPONSE PROTOCOL

INTRODUCTION

This document outlines The Standard Response Protocol (SRP) and offers guidance on incorporating this protocol into a school safety plan for critical incident response within individual schools in a school district.

"SRP is not a replacement... it's an enhancement to your existing safety plans."

The intent of this document is to provide basic guidance with respect for local conditions and authorities. The only mandate presented is that districts, agencies and departments retain the "Terms of Art, which are actions," and "Directives" defined by this protocol.

The SRP is not a replacement for any school safety plan or program. It is simply a classroom response enhancement for critical incidents, designed to provide consistent, clear, shared language and actions among all students, staff and first responders.

As a standard, SRP is being adopted by emergency managers, law enforcement, school and district administrators and emergency medical services across the country. Hundreds of agencies have evaluated the SRP and recommended the SRP to thousands of schools across the US and Canada.

New materials and updates can be found online at http://iloveuguys.org.

A CRITICAL LOOK

Be prepared to look at existing plans with a critical eye, as often they can be described as a "Directive" of a certain "Term of Art." For example, conducting a fire drill is practicing a specific type of evacuation and the actions performed are similar in all evacuation scenarios. It makes sense to teach and train broader evacuation techniques while testing or practicing a more specific directive, like evacuating to the parking lot due to a fire.

TIME BARRIERS

Time barriers or measures taken beforehand to 'harden the structure' can be an invaluable asset to safety; not only for staff and students, but also visitors to a campus who expect a friendly and secure environment.

Time barriers are best described as a physical barrier that slows down the entry into, or movement through, a facility. Any additional delay allows trained persons to take further protective action and gives first responders more time to arrive.

An example of a time barrier is making the exterior doors of a building automatically lock, and could include installing a film on glass door panels to prevent them from shattering, thereby delaying an intruder's attempt to break into the premises.

Finally, the most powerful time barrier in an active assailant event is a locked classroom door. The Sandy Hook Advisory Commission Report* says this:

"The testimony and other evidence presented to the Commission reveals that there has never been an event in which an active shooter breached a locked classroom door."

In Foundation investigations of past school shootings where life was lost behind a locked classroom door, some edge cases were revealed. The perpetrator in the Red Lake, MN incident gained entry into the classroom by breaking through the side panel windows next to the classroom door. In the Platte Canyon hostage incident, the perpetrator was already in the room when Jeffco Regional SWAT explosively breached the classroom door. At Marjory Stoneman Douglas High School, shots were fired through glass panels in doors, but the perpetrator never entered any classrooms.

*FINAL REPORT OF THE SANDY HOOK ADVISORY COMMISSION
Presented to Governor Dannel P. Malloy State of Connecticut
March 6, 2015
Document page 238 - Appendix A-I.1

BEFORE YOU BEGIN

Districts and schools typically have a comprehensive safety program established and executed by a dedicated team of safety or security personnel. That same Safety Team should be responsible for incorporating the SRP into the safety plan. Including staff, students and a counselor or nurse on the Safety Team can greatly increase the buy-in and participation from all campus safety stakeholders.

If it was not done during the development of the existing safety plan it is highly encouraged that, while incorporating the SRP, the safety team establish contact with local emergency services and law enforcement officials as they can help ensure safety plans will not conflict with existing local emergency services protocols.

THE STANDARD RESPONSE PROTOCOL

A critical ingredient in the safe school recipe is the uniform classroom response to an incident at school. Weather events, fires, accidents, intruders and other threats to student safety are scenarios that are planned and trained for by school and district administration and staff.

Historically, schools have taken a scenario-based approach to respond to hazards and threats. It's not uncommon to find a stapled sheaf of papers or tabbed binder in a teacher's desk that describes a variety of things that might happen, and the specific response to each event.

SRP IS ACTION BASED

The Standard Response Protocol is based not on individual scenarios but on the response to any given scenario. Like the Incident Command System (ICS), SRP demands a specific vocabulary but also allows for great flexibility. The premise is simple: there are five specific actions that can be performed during an incident. When communicating these actions, the action is labeled with a "Term of Art" and is then followed by a "Directive." Execution of the action is performed by active participants, including students, staff, teachers and first responders.

1. **Hold** is followed by "In your Room or Area. Clear the Halls" and is the protocol used when the hallways need to be kept clear of people.
2. **Secure** is followed by "Get Inside, Lock Outside Doors" and is the protocol used to safeguard students and staff within the building.
3. **Lockdown** is followed by "Locks, Lights, Out of Sight" and is the protocol used to secure individual rooms and keep students quiet and in place.
4. **Evacuate** may be followed by a location, and is the protocol used to move students and staff from one location to a different location in or out of the building.
5. **Shelter** is always followed by the hazard and a safety strategy and is the protocol for group and self protection.

These specific actions can act as both a verb and a noun. If the action is Lockdown, it would be announced on public address as "Lockdown! Locks, Lights, Out of Sight." Communication to local responders would then be "We are under Lockdown."

ACTIONS

Each response has specific student and staff actions. The Evacuate response might be followed by a location: "Evacuate to the Bus Zone." Responses can also be chained. For instance, "Evacuate to Hallway. Shelter for Earthquake. Drop, Cover and Hold."

BENEFITS

The benefits of SRP become quickly apparent. By standardizing the vocabulary, all stakeholders can understand the response and status of the event. For students, this provides continuity of expectations and actions throughout their educational career. For teachers, this becomes a simpler process to train and drill. For first responders, the common vocabulary and protocols establish a greater predictability that persists through the duration of an incident. Parents can easily understand the practices and can reinforce the protocol. Additionally, this protocol enables rapid response determination when an unforeseen event occurs.

The protocol also allows for a more predictable series of actions as an event unfolds. An intruder event may start as a Lockdown, but as the intruder is isolated, first responders would assist as parts of the school go to an "Evacuate to the gym and Lockdown," and later "Evacuate to the bus zone."

SECURE VS. LOCKDOWN

The differentiation between Secure and Lockdown is a critical element in SRP. Secure recovers people from outside the building, secures the building perimeter and locks all exterior doors. This would be implemented when there is a threat or hazard outside of the building. Criminal activity, dangerous events in the community, or even a vicious dog on the playground would be examples of a Secure response. While the Secure response encourages greater staff situational awareness, it allows for educational practices to continue with little classroom interruption or distraction.

Lockdown is a classroom-based protocol that requires locking the classroom door, turning off the lights and placing students out of sight of any corridor windows. Student action during Lockdown is to remain quiet. It does not mandate locking exterior doors for a few reasons: risk is increased to students or staff in exposed areas attempting to lock the doors, and locking exterior doors inhibits entry of first responders and increases risk as responders attempt to breach doors. If the doors are already locked, leave them alone.

Be aware that situations can change quickly. Depending on what's happening, a Lockdown might change to a Secure condition, or the Secure condition evolves to Lockdown. Refer to the FAQs on page 30.

TACTICAL RESPONSES

SRP also acknowledges that some school incidents involve a tactical response from law enforcement, and suggests consultation with local law enforcement regarding expectations and actions.

STANDARD RESPONSE PROTOCOL

PROTOCOL DETAILS SUMMARY

This section of the guidance defines conditions, actions, responsibilities and other aspects of preparing and incorporating The Standard Response Protocol within a school or district safety plan.

PREREQUISITES: NIMS AND ICS

In order to coordinate the use of the SRP in district plans, it is highly recommended that key individuals within the district and those with a role in district/campus emergency operations, complete the following courses through FEMA.

1. IS 100.C: Introduction to the Incident Command System
2. IS-700.B: An Introduction to the National Incident Management System
3. IS 362.A: Multihazard Emergency Planning for Schools

These courses are available online, at no cost using the web at http://training.fema.gov. Anticipate 1 to 3 hours per course to successfully achieve certification. The courses are offered at no charge. Please note: The "I Love U Guys" Foundation is not affiliated with FEMA.

RESOURCES AND CREATING RELATIONSHIPS

Throughout this book, you'll see quite a few suggestions to contact your local or regional responders, whether it's law enforcement, emergency services or fire departments. Communication with these local resources is essential.

In most areas, schools are the largest population centers during a school day, so it makes sense to utilize the advice and services those agencies provide. Additionally, some county emergency managers are equipped to assist with your safety planning. Some school districts are even able to engage with their regional Department of Homeland Security for training resources.

Take a look around your county and state and see what's available.

If you would like to speak with other schools or districts prior to utilizing the Standard Response Protocol, contact The " I Love U Guys" Foundation (info@iloveuguys.org) and we may be able to connect you with a school or district near you that has a similar profile and similar challenges.

DOORS, LOCKS AND STRESS

A consistent observation by first responders is that human beings have difficulty completing even routine tasks when they are under stress. The otherwise simple task of locking the classroom door may become extremely difficult for a teacher who has just heard a Lockdown order. Elevated adrenaline levels may result in the loss of fine motor skills, which can impede an act as normal as inserting a key to lock a door.

Keeping classroom doors locked during instruction has proven to be a time barrier. While this may create an inconvenience if students are late or need to re-enter classroom for other reasons, it provides an essential layer of protection against intruders.

TALK TO THE FIRE MARSHAL

It's important to discuss classroom security options and modification with local fire authorities. Some will allow a locked classroom door to be propped open during the school day, while some will not. Variances in local Fire Codes and application will help determine the options for your schools.

MEMORANDA OF UNDERSTANDING

Establishing a Memorandum of Understanding (MOU) and/or Mutual Aid Agreement (MAA) between responding agencies and local resources are critical. It is insufficient to rely on a conversation or handshake between entities who would respond to an incident or provide resources during an emergency.

Written agreements such as MOUs and MAAs are important to emergency operation plans and should be reviewed and updated regularly.

An SRP-focused Sample MOU between a School District and Law Enforcement/Fire/EMS was created by The "I Love U Guys" Foundation in order to guide schools in creating effective MOU's with local first responders. This can be downloaded from The "I Love U Guys" Foundation's website.

CLASSROOM POSTERS

Part of a school's commitment to SRP is displaying posters in classrooms, libraries, cafeterias, gymnasiums, auditoriums and hallways.

The Foundation recognizes that this commitment may impact printing budgets and consequently asks that schools or districts commit to a time frame when poster installation can be completed.

Two sizes of posters are available in English and Spanish at http://iloveuguys.org at no charge.

TRAINING RESOURCES

While the SRP materials may be downloaded and implemented at no cost, The Foundation can provide on-site or online training for a cost, and has worked with a number of organizations in providing training workshops.

Send training inquiries to training@iloveuguys.org.

IN AN EMERGENCY
TAKE ACTION

HOLD! In your room or area. Clear the halls.

STUDENTS
Remain in the area until the "All Clear" is indicated

ADULTS
Close and lock door
Business as usual
Account for students and adults

SECURE! Get inside. Lock outside doors.

STUDENTS
Return inside
Business as usual

ADULTS
Bring everyone indoors
Lock outside doors
Increase situational awareness
Business as usual
Account for students and adults

LOCKDOWN! Locks, lights, out of sight.

STUDENTS
Move away from sight
Maintain silence
Do not open the door

ADULTS
Lock interior doors
Turn out the lights
Move away from sight
Do not open the door
Maintain silence
Account for students and adults
Prepare to evade or defend

EVACUATE! (A location may be specified)

STUDENTS
Evacuate to specified location
Bring your phone
Instructions may be provided about retaining or leaving belongings

ADULTS
Lead evacuation to specified location
Account for students and adults
Notify if missing, extra or injured students or adults

SHELTER! Hazard and safety strategy.

STUDENTS

Hazard	Safety Strategy
Tornado	Evacuate to shelter area
Hazmat	Seal the room
Earthquake	Drop, cover and hold
Tsunami	Get to high ground

ADULTS
Lead safety strategy
Account for students and adults

STANDARD RESPONSE PROTOCOL

COMMUNICATION

Every school's Emergency Operations Plan (EOP) should contain a section for communicating both internally and externally during a crisis situation.

In any type of event, clear and well-planned communication is essential. Depending on the type of incident, you might have only minutes to prepare a statement and communicate it to the appropriate people.

Primarily, give the staff and students as much information as possible so they can make informed decisions about their actions. If little is known about the situation, tell them that.

Communication to parents and guardians is critical as well. It's likely that a number of them will show up at the school no matter what's going on, so letting them know what's happening and what to do is a must.

INCIDENT COMMAND

When your Safety Team is creating an EOP, they'll include some level of the Incident Command System (ICS), which is the hierarchy of authority and responsibilities. One role in ICS is the Public Information Officer (PIO) and this role can be used on a daily basis.

Having a Communication Team in place in your school and/or district is good practice in order to keep lines of communication ongoing for everyday events and activities.

Many school districts have a full time Communication/PIO representative. Within a school, there is usually at least one person who manages the low level event and activity communication along with their primary job.

High level event information should be handled by a competent and well versed individual who provides information that is clear, concise and complete enough in content to further the mission.

Create a policy for protocol and content for each communication channel to maintain consistency.

CHANNELS

Decide which methods of communication are the best fit for your community. This is reliant on your community's internet bandwidth and preferences. Whatever you choose needs to be reliable, fast, and reach a high percentage of the community members. Document who on the Communication Team has access to update each channel.

Also, think about which channels are used regularly for day to day messaging, like emails, and consider using alternate methods for emergencies such as text and phone, which may not be used as frequently. Doing so will alert

the recipients that this is not the regular, daily email, but something more important.

CONTACTS

After determining the best channels to use, decide who you will need to communicate with. Certainly staff and parents, but also students depending on the age group. Asking parents to keep their contact information updated is critical. Add responders and dispatchers as needed.

TIME

For certain incidents there are only a few minutes to prepare. If Law Enforcement or Fire is involved, people will hear about an incident quickly. Reaching your stakeholders immediately with any type of message acknowledging the incident is essential. Have some basic message formats approved and ready to use.

CONTENT

Not every situation needs immediate text messages and emails, so it's important to determine what is warranted and when. Less urgent situations—a school cancellation with ample notice, for example—might warrant an email, mass phone message and website update, whereas an unexpectedly early dismissal requires mass phone calls and text messages to ensure that information is received quickly.

An initial message can be as simple as stating that something has happened, and telling stakeholders where to find updates.

Include only the factual information you have; do not speculate. The recipients of your outgoing messages must be able to trust in the validity of the content.

Any situation that requires emergency communication for an incident will also require a follow-up.

PREPARATION

A tabletop exercise is a start; basically it's a brainstorming session. Your Communication Team can talk through possible scenarios and formulate messaging accordingly. They must think about what immediate information is necessary, how to follow up, and who they will need to speak with/follow to receive trusted updates.

Use the 27/9/3 rule during message preparation. This is a very basic recommendation and suggests using a total of 27 words, which can be spoken in about 9 seconds, containing three or fewer key points.

The team should pre-script some basic messages that may be sent out, with blank spaces for details like time and date. Having these pre-approved and available will aid the team later if they're under stress or time constraints.

HOLD
In Your Room or Area

HOLD
IN YOUR ROOM OR AREA.
CLEAR THE HALLS

There may be situations that require students to remain in their classrooms. For example, an altercation in the hallway may require keeping students out of the halls until it is resolved. A medical issue may require only one area to be cleared, with halls still open in case outside medical assistance is required.

There may be a need for students who are not in a classroom to proceed to an area where they can be supervised and remain safe.

PUBLIC ADDRESS

The public address for Hold is: "Hold in your room or area. Clear the Halls." and is repeated twice each time the public address is performed. There may be a need to add directives for students that are not in a classroom, at lunch or some other location where they should remain until the hold is lifted.

"Hold in your room or area. Clear the Halls.
 Hold in your room or area. Clear the Halls."

PUBLIC ADDRESS - RELEASE

A Hold can be released by Public Address.

"The Hold is released. All Clear.
 The Hold is released. All Clear."

INCIDENT COMMAND SYSTEM

The School Incident Command System should be initiated.

ACTIONS

Students and teachers are to remain in their classroom or area, even if there is a scheduled class change, until the all clear is announced.

Students and staff in common areas, like a cafeteria or a gym, may be asked to remain in those areas or move to adjoining areas like a locker room.

Students and staff outside of the building should remain outside unless administration directs otherwise.

It is suggested that prior to locking the classroom door, teachers should rapidly sweep the hallway for nearby students. Additionally, teachers should take attendance, note the time, and conduct business as usual.

In a high school with an open campus policy, communicate as much detail as possible to students who temporarily off campus.

RESPONSIBILITY

Typically an administrator is responsible for initiating a Hold, however anyone should be able to call for a Hold if they observe something happening that would require this action.

PREPARATION

Student, teacher, and administrator training.

DRILLS

Hold should be drilled at least once a year, or as mandated by state requirements.

CONTINGENCIES

Students are trained that if they are not in a classroom they may be asked to identify the nearest classroom and join that class for the duration of the Hold.

EXAMPLES OF HOLD CONDITIONS

The following are some examples of when a school might initiate a Hold:

- An altercation in a hallway;
- A medical issue that need attention;
- Unfinished maintenance operation in a common area during class changes.

INTERNAL/PRINCIPAL MESSAGING

To students and staff during an incident.

Example Situation: Medical Emergency

"Students and staff, please Hold in the cafeteria or your room. We're attending to a medical situation near the office."

"Students and staff, the Hold is released. All clear. Thank you for your assistance with making this Hold work smoothly."

MESSAGING TO PARENTS

To parent and community after a Hold event

Example Situation: Medical Emergency

"Today at (**time of day**), there was a limited First Aid event in the building which required the Hold action to be initiated. Hallways were cleared and the event was handled promptly. Questions can be directed to (**PIO**) jdoe@school.org"

SECURE
Get Inside, Lock Outside Doors.

SECURE
GET INSIDE, LOCK OUTSIDE DOORS.

The Secure Protocol is called when there is a threat or hazard outside of the school building. Whether it's due to violence or criminal activity in the immediate neighborhood, or a dangerous animal in the playground, Secure uses the security of the physical facility to act as protection.

PUBLIC ADDRESS

The public address for Secure is: "Secure! Get Inside. Lock outside doors" and is repeated twice each time the public address is performed.

"Secure! Get Inside, Lock outside doors.
Secure! Get Inside, Lock outside doors."

ACTIONS

The Secure Protocol demands bringing people into a secure building, and locking all outside access points.

Where possible, classroom activities would continue uninterrupted. Classes being held outside would return to the building and, if possible, continue inside the building.

There may be occasions when students expect to be able to leave the building - end of classes, job commitment, etc. Depending on the condition, this may have to be delayed until the area is safe.

During the training period, it should be emphasized to students as well as their parents that they may be inconvenienced by these directives, but their cooperation is important to ensure their safety.

CONTROLLED RELEASE

Circumstances where a threat is perceived but not directly evident may warrant a Controlled Release. During a Controlled Release, parents or guardians may be asked to pick up students rather than have them walk home. Buses may run as normal, but increased monitoring of the bus area would occur. There may be additional law enforcement presence.

MONITORED ENTRY

When there is a perceived threat but it's not immediate, anyone entering the building is more closely monitored, especially during after school gatherings. Students changing classes between buildings or going to the parking lot might be escorted with a heightened awareness.

INCIDENT COMMAND SYSTEM

The School Incident Command System should be initiated.

RESPONSIBILITY

During a Secure event, administration or staff may be required to lock exterior access points. Staff members assigned "Primary Responsibility" for a "Secure Zone" would follow the designated protocol during a drill as well. These areas may include doorways, windows, loading docks, and fire escape ladder access points. The assigned staff is designated as having "Secure Duty."

A person should also be assigned "Secondary Responsibility" for Secure Duty in the event the person with Primary Responsibility is absent or unable to perform the protocol.

Someone should be assigned to attach the Secure posters (shown on the right), outfacing, to building entry doors to alert potential visitors of the Secure condition.

REPORTED BY

Secure is typically reported by emergency dispatch to the school office. Office staff then invokes the public address and informs administration.

It may also be reported by students, staff or teachers if a threat is directly observed outside of the building.

PREPARATION

Identification of perimeter access points that must be locked in a Secure event defines the Perimeter. In the event a perimeter cannot be secured, identify areas within each building that can be secured.

Secure Zones - areas of a school or campus with exterior access points - should be established and protocols developed to ensure that those on "Secure Duty" secure all areas in their zone.

Preparation includes identification of staff with Primary and Secondary responsibility and assignment of these duties.

DRILLS

Secure drills should be performed at least twice a year, or as mandated by state requirements. At least one should be performed while outdoor activities are in progress.

CONTINGENCIES

There may be physical attributes to the campus that mandate special handling of a Secure event. An example would be a campus where modular buildings are present. If the modular building cannot be secured, it may be best for students to Evacuate to the main building rather than going to Secure in the modular building. Listen for specific additional directives.

If the school is a distributed campus (multiple permanent buildings), they will have to consider what their perimeter is. In a perceived and indirect threat, they may decide that extra supervision for class changes between buildings is sufficient and appropriate.

If, during a Secure event, an additional hazard manifests (i.e.: fire, flood, hazmat), then additional directives will be given for the appropriate response.

EXAMPLES OF SECURE CONDITIONS

The following are some examples of when a school or emergency dispatch might call for Secure Protocol.

- Unknown or unauthorized person on the grounds
- Dangerous animal on school grounds
- Criminal activity in area
- Planned police activity in the neighborhood

MEDIA MESSAGING

To the community during an event.

Example Situation: Criminal Activity Nearby

If your school has been notified by law enforcement that there's activity in the area, you might use this type of message:

"We have been advised there is police activity in the area of (**location**). Staff and students are accounted for and the Secure Protocol has been established. Updates to follow."

DISPATCH MESSAGING

To the school prior to this occurring.

Example Situation: Planned Warrant Service Notification

"Be advised there is a planned police activity today (**date**), sometime between (**time range**), in the area of (**neighborhood or nearby intersection**). We request the schools in the area place their campuses in the Secure protocol during this event. Be advised there may be an increased Law Enforcement presence in the area and the potential of loud noises. We will notify you when the event has concluded."

WHEN... THEN...

The following scenario happened in a school district, and is a good topic of discussion during tabletop exercises.

Example: Shots are fired in the neighborhood

In this event, the school day had ended at a neighborhood middle school. Some students were walking home, some were on buses, and some were on campus for after-school sports. When the shots were fired, who was in charge of the communication?

- Law Enforcement needed to alert the school.
- The school was responsible for sending an alert to students/parents/guardians.
- Students who were still on campus were brought inside, and the campus enacted the Secure Protocol.
- Law Enforcement increased patrols in the neighborhood as they sought the source of the gunfire.
- Dispatch maintained communication with the school's Communication Team.

LOCKDOWN
Locks, Lights, Out of Sight

LOCKDOWN
LOCKS, LIGHTS, OUT OF SIGHT
Lockdown is called when there is a threat or hazard inside the school building. From parental custody disputes to intruders to an active assailant, Lockdown uses classroom and school security actions to protect students and staff from the threat.

PUBLIC ADDRESS
The public address for Lockdown is: "Lockdown! Locks, Lights, Out of Sight!" and is repeated twice each time the public address is performed.

"Lockdown! Locks, Lights, Out of Sight!
Lockdown! Locks, Lights, Out of Sight!"

ACTIONS
The Lockdown protocol demands locking individual classroom doors, offices and other securable areas, moving occupants out of line of sight of corridor windows, turning off lights to make the room seem unoccupied, and having occupants maintain silence.

There is no call to action to lock the building's exterior access points. Rather, the protocol advises leaving the perimeter as is. The reasoning is simple - sending staff to lock outside doors exposes them to unnecessary risk and inhibits first responders' entry into the building. If the exterior doors are already locked, leave them locked but do have a conversation with your local responders so they understand and can gain access during a Lockdown. The best option is to have the ability to lock doors remotely.

Teacher, staff and student training reinforces the practice of not opening the classroom door once in Lockdown. No indication of occupancy should be revealed until first responders open the door.

If the location of the threat is apparent and people do not have the option to get behind a door, it is appropriate to self-evacuate away from the threat.

INCIDENT COMMAND SYSTEM
The School Incident Command System should be initiated.

RESPONSIBILITY
The classroom teacher is responsible for implementing their classroom Lockdown. If it is safe to do so, the teacher should gather students into the classroom prior to locking door. The teacher should lock all classroom access points and facilitate moving occupants out of sight.

REPORTED BY
When there is a life safety threat on campus, a Lockdown should be immediately initiated by any student or staff member. Initiating the Lockdown may happen through various methods, or a combination of methods, depending on the procedures and alert systems utilized by each school and district. Lockdown alerts may be made by word of mouth, phone, radio systems, intercom, panic buttons, or even more advanced forms of technology. Plan the communication method in advance to set expectations for students and staff. Regardless of the method(s) of alert notification, the initiation of a Lockdown should be consistent, simple and swift, and include immediate notification of school administration and local law enforcement agencies.

PREPARATION
Identification of classroom access points that must be locked in the event of a Lockdown is essential preparation. These may include doorways, windows, loading docks, and fire escape ladder access points.

A "safe zone" should also be identified within the classroom that is out of sight of the corridor window. Teachers and students should be trained to not open the classroom door, leaving a first responder, school safety team member or school administrator to unlock it.

Students, staff and teachers should be advised that a Lockdown may persist for several hours, and during an incident silence is recommended.

DRILLS
Lockdown drills should be performed at least twice a year, or as mandated by state requirements. If possible one of these drills should be performed with local law enforcement personnel participation. At a minimum, law enforcement participation in the drill should occur no less than once every two years.

For more information, see the Lockdown Drills section of this book.

CONTINGENCIES
Students and staff who are outside of classrooms when a Lockdown is announced should try to get into the closest available classroom, or room with door that can be secured. In the event someone cannot get into a room before doors are locked, they should be instructed about other options. In this situation, students and staff should be trained to hide or even evacuate themselves away from the building or area. Students and staff should receive training on where to go if they evacuate, so they can be safe and accounted for.

If, during a Lockdown, an additional hazard manifests inside the school such as a fire, flood, or hazmat incident, then situational decisions must be made. There should be discussions about reacting to a fire alarm if it is activated during a Lockdown. This may require following additional directives of the SRP.

CELL PHONES

It is not uncommon for school administrators to ban cell phone use during a Lockdown. Parent instincts may be at odds with that ban. Often, one of the first things a parent will do when there is a crisis in the school is text their child.

In evaluating actual Lockdown events, the initial crisis may only take minutes. After the threat is mitigated, Law Enforcement typically clears the school one classroom at a time. This process may take significant time. During this time, both parents and students can reduce stress through text communications. This also provides a classroom management strategy. Selecting three or four students at time, a teacher may ask students to text their parents with a message like this: "We're in Lockdown. I'm OK and I'll update you every 5 minutes." Certainly, if a threat is imminent, texting would be discouraged.

There is also an opportunity to ask the students to text their parents with crafted messages as an event unfolds. For example, "Pick me up at Lincoln Elementary in one hour. Bring your ID," might be recommended for student-parent reunification.

It may also be beneficial to have students turn off both Wi-Fi and cellular data services. This frees up bandwidth for first responders, while still allowing SMS text messaging.

EXAMPLES OF LOCKDOWN CONDITIONS

The following are a few examples of when a school or emergency dispatch might call for a Lockdown.

- Dangerous animal within school building
- Intruder
- Dangerous and violent parent or student
- Report of a weapon
- Active assailant

RED CARD/GREEN CARD

Red Card/Green Cards should NOT be used for a Lockdown. Based on a number of tactical assessments, the overwhelming consensus is that this practice provides information to an armed intruder that there are potential targets in that room.

MEDIA MESSAGING

To community after an event.

Example Situation: Intruder in the School

"Today at (**time of day**), there was an individual observed entering (**school name**). The individual was later identified as a non-custodial parent of a student at (**school name**). School officials placed the school on Lockdown and notified the police of the situation. The individual was not able to gain access to any students at the school and the police are investigating the situation."

DISPATCH

To responding officers during an event.

Example Situation: Angry/Violent Parent at School

"(**Dispatched units**) there is a disturbance at (**school name**). A parent (**identity if known, physical description**) on scene is screaming, throwing items, and threatening staff in the office area of the school. The reporting party advised the school has been placed on Lockdown. (**time stamp**)."

LAW ENFORCEMENT MESSAGING

To community/media after event.

Example Situation: Weapon Report

"On (**date**) at (**time of day**), (**LE Agency**) received the report of a student who had brought a weapon to (**school name**) and was allegedly armed in an otherwise unoccupied classroom. School officials advised the remainder of the school had been placed on Lockdown. Upon arrival, officers were able to make contact with the student and placed the student into custody without incident. The investigation is ongoing."

THE DURATION OF A LOCKDOWN

A question that occasionally arises is "How long does it take to release a Lockdown?" The answer is, "That depends, but probably longer than you want to hear."

The Foundation has heard accounts of a Lockdown lasting for hours. In one case - a weapon report - the school was in Lockdown for over three hours. In another, an active assailant in the building, it took about an hour after the issue was resolved for law enforcement to clear the classrooms.

Some schools have created Lockdown kits. A five gallon bucket, kitty litter, and a shower curtain to accommodate the potential of being unable to use a restroom.

WHAT ABOUT CELL PHONES?

One of the occasionally heated conversations is about cell phone usage. If the current trends continue, there will be a point in the future where nearly every student will have a device.

There may be cases where law enforcement will ask students to leave their phones behind. A bomb threat for example.

In many cases, having the ability to craft messages for students to send their parents, or for students to call their parents, can be of tremendous value.

The Foundation freely admits to a bias though. Take just a moment and think of the origination of the Foundation. (See page 9.)

EVACUATE
A Location may also be given

EVACUATE TO A LOCATION
Evacuate is called when there is a need to move people from one location to another.

Most often, evacuations will be necessary when there's a heating/ventilation system failure, gas leak, or bomb threat in the area. In those cases, people will be allowed to bring their personal items with them. An evacuation drill is very similar to a fire drill.

PUBLIC ADDRESS
The public address for Evacuate is: "Evacuate! To a Location" and is repeated twice each time the public address is performed. For instance, "Evacuate! To the Flag Pole."

"Evacuate! To a location.
Evacuate! To a location."

ACTIONS
The Evacuate Protocol demands students and staff move in an orderly fashion.

INCIDENT COMMAND SYSTEM
The School Incident Command System should be initiated.

RESPONSIBILITY
The classroom teacher or administrator is usually responsible for initiating an evacuation. The directives or actions may vary for fire, bomb threat, or other emergency. In a Police Led Evacuation, students may be instructed to form a single file line and hold hands front and back, or students and staff may be asked to put their hands on their heads while evacuating. Other directions may be invoked during an evacuation and student and staff should be prepared to follow specific instructions given by staff or first responders.

PREPARATION
Evacuation preparation involves the identification of facility evacuation routes, evacuation assembly points and evacuation sites, as well as student, teacher, and administrator training. An evacuation site usually becomes the reunification site, so plan accordingly. Ideally choose an offsite evacuation facility that's in walking distance and another father away from the school in case the hazard is in the immediate area. Have an MOU in place with each site to outline expectations and responsibilities in advance. There is a sample MOU for this on The "I Love U Guys" website.

EVACUATION ASSEMBLY
The Evacuation Assembly refers to gathering at the Evacuation Assembly Point(s). Teachers are instructed to take roll after arrival at the Evacuation Assembly Point(s).

Schools with large populations might plan on having multiple, predetermined assembly points so everyone isn't grouped together.

DRILLS
Evacuation drills should be performed at least twice a year or as mandated by state law. Fire drills are required monthly in schools and constitute a valid evacuation drill.

INCIDENT COMMAND SYSTEM
The School Incident Command System should be initiated.

CONTINGENCIES
Students are trained that if they are separated from their class during an evacuation, then joining another evacuation line is acceptable. They should be instructed to identify themselves to the teacher in their group after arriving at the Evacuation Site.

RED CARD/GREEN CARD/MED CARD
After taking roll the Red/Green/Med Card system is employed for administration or first responders to quickly, visually identify the status of the teachers' classes. Teachers will hold up the Green card if they have all their students and are good to go. They hold up Red card if they are missing students, extra students or another problem, and use the Med card to indicate their need for some sort of medical attention.

See the Materials Section for examples.

INTERNAL PRINCIPAL / SRO MESSAGING
To the students and staff.

Example Situation: Possible Hazmat Situation in the School

"Evacuate to your assembly point. Evacuate to your assembly point. Please initiate evacuation procedures immediately and meet at your assigned assembly point outside"

MEDIA MESSAGING
To the media/community after an event.

Example Situation: Gas Leak

"Today at (**time of day**) students and staff at (**school name**) were ordered to evacuate due to the report of the smell of natural gas in the area of the school. The students evacuated to (**evacuation location**) in order to be reunited with their parents/guardians. Officials say the natural gas odor was as a result of a gas line that was broken by a road crew at (**location**) and is currently being repaired. School will be back in session on its normal schedule tomorrow."

POLICE LED
Evacuation After a Lockdown

POLICE LED EVACUATION
In the rare situations where law enforcement is clearing classrooms and escorting students and staff out of the classroom and through the building, it is important to have provided advance instruction on what to expect.

PUBLIC ADDRESS
There may or may not be any public address notifying students and staff that law enforcement is performing these actions.

ACTIONS
As officers enter the classroom, students and staff must keep their hands visible and empty. It is unlikely that students or staff may be able to bring backpacks, purses or any personal items with them during a Police Led Evacuation.

WHAT TO EXPECT
Prepare students and staff that during a Police Led Evacuation, officers may be loud, direct and commanding. Students and staff may also be searched both in the classroom and again at the assembly area.

EMOTIONAL RESPONSIBILITY
There is a new conversation occurring with law enforcement regarding their role in post-event recovery. This is a growing area and warrants conversations between schools, districts, and agencies about how to keep students safe, and reduce trauma that might be associated with a Police Led Evacuation.

PREPARATION
Student, teacher, and administrator training.

CONTINGENCIES
Depending on the situation, Incident Commanders should consider leaving students and staff in their rooms until transportation arrives. Your team can also discuss communicating to classrooms that the threat has been minimized enough that they may relax and wait for evacuation.

When it's time, each room can be cleared directly to the buses in order to minimize trauma.

It is recommended to avoid the scene of the incident when exiting. Transport directly to the Reunification Site.

MEDIA MESSAGING
To the media/community after an event.

Example Situation: Violent Event

"On (**date**) at (**time of day**), (**agency name**) responded to (**school name**) in reference to (**event type**). Officers assisted with safely escorting students and staff out of the school and to the Evacuation site where the (**School District**) was able to initiate the Reunification process."

DISPATCH MESSAGING
To responding officers during an event.

Example Situation: Police Led Evacuation

"(**Dispatched Units**) respond to (**school name**) to assist with Evacuation of students and staff. Assistance is needed to accompany individuals out of the school and to the Secure Assembly Area at (**location**). Respond to the Command Post for your assignment. (**time stamp**)"

LAW ENFORCEMENT MESSAGING
To responding officers during an event.

Example Situation: Gas Leak

(**Police unit name**) respond to (**area near the school)** to assist with evacuating students from (**school name**) because of gas smell in the building. Meet with (**supervisor**) for further information to assist with Evacuation and Reunification.

SHELTER
State the Hazard and Safety Strategy

SHELTER
Shelter is called when specific protective actions are needed based on a threat or hazard. Training should include response to threats such as tornado, earthquake , hazardous materials situation or other local threats.

PUBLIC ADDRESS
The public address for shelter should include the hazard and the safety strategy. The public address is repeated twice each time the public address is performed.

"Shelter! For a hazard. Using safety strategy. Shelter! For a hazard. Using safety strategy."

HAZARDS MAY INCLUDE
- Tornado
- Severe weather
- Wildfires
- Flooding
- Hazmat spill or release
- Earthquake
- Tsunami

SAFETY STRATEGIES MAY INCLUDE
- Evacuate to shelter area
- Seal the room
- Drop, cover and hold
- Get to high ground

ACTIONS
Collaboration with local responders, the National Weather Service, and other local, regional and state resources will help in developing specific actions for your district response.

INCIDENT COMMAND SYSTEM
The School Incident Command System should be initiated.

RESPONSIBILITY
Sheltering requires that all students and staff follow response directives. Districts should have procedures for all foreseeable local hazards and threats which include provisions for those individuals with access and functional needs.

PREPARATION
Identification and marking of facility shelter areas.

DRILLS
Shelter safety strategies should be drilled at least twice a year, or as mandated by the state.

SHELTER - STATE THE HAZARD AND SAFETY STRATEGY
Using the Shelter Protocol and stating the hazard allows for understanding of the threat and the associated protective actions. Most often, the Shelter Protocol is utilized for tornadoes and other severe weather, in which case it would include the shelter location for students and staff, and what protective posture or action they should take.

Sheltering for a Hazmat spill or release is very different. In the case of a Hazmat situation, students and staff would be directed to close their windows, shut down their heating and air conditioning units and seal windows and doors to preserve the good inside air while restricting the entry of any contaminated outside air. Listening to specific directives is critical to a successful emergency response.

PLAIN LANGUAGE
NIMS and ICS require the use of plain language. Codes and specific language that are not readily understood by the general public are no longer to be used. The SRP uses shared, plain, natural language between students, staff and first responders. If there are specific directives that need to be issued for a successful response in a school, those should be made clearly using plain language. There is nothing wrong with adding additional directives as to where to shelter, or what protective actions should be used in the response.

CUSTOMIZATION
The classroom poster is sufficient for generic Shelter guidance. The Foundation recognizes that localized hazards may need to be added to the poster. For this reason, the Public Address poster is available in MS Word for customization.

ABOUT SHELTER-IN-PLACE
There is a long tradition of using the term "Shelter-in-place" for a variety of hazards. While still in common use, the SRP suggests simply stating the hazard and providing a safety strategy.

A deep exploration of the FEMA website found over a dozen different scenarios where "Shelter-in-place" was advised. Two of the most common were for Tornado or Hazmat. Very different actions would be taken for those hazards. A single directive, "Shelter-in-place" doesn't provide the necessary information. "Tornado! Get to the storm shelter! " is more direct.

MATERIALS
AND NOTE TO PRINTER

SRP OVERVIEW WALL POSTER

This K12 SRP overview wall poster was created for you to print and place on walls in order to remind everyone of the different SRP actions and allow teachers to start the conversation about SRP with their students.

Placing Posters is an essential step in full implementation of the SRP. The poster should be displayed in every classroom, near building entries, and the entrances to the cafeteria, auditorium and gym. The shelter hazards and safety strategies can be modified for local conditions.

The poster is available in letter size (8.5 x 11") and tabloid size (11 x 17"), in English and Spanish.

IN AN EMERGENCY
TAKE ACTION

HOLD! In your room or area. Clear the halls.

STUDENTS
Remain in the area until the "All Clear" is indicated

ADULTS
Close and lock door
Business as usual
Account for students and adults

SECURE! Get inside. Lock outside doors.

STUDENTS
Return inside
Business as usual

ADULTS
Bring everyone indoors
Lock outside doors
Increase situational awareness
Business as usual
Account for students and adults

LOCKDOWN! Locks, lights, out of sight.

STUDENTS
Move away from sight
Maintain silence
Do not open the door

ADULTS
Lock interior doors
Turn out the lights
Move away from sight
Do not open the door
Maintain silence
Account for students and adults
Prepare to evade or defend

EVACUATE! (A location may be specified)

STUDENTS
Evacuate to specified location
Bring your phone
Instructions may be provided about retaining or leaving belongings

ADULTS
Lead evacuation to specified location
Account for students and adults
Notify if missing, extra or injured students or adults

SHELTER! Hazard and safety strategy.

STUDENTS

Hazard	Safety Strategy
Tornado	Evacuate to shelter area
Hazmat	Seal the room
Earthquake	Drop, cover and hold
Tsunami	Get to high ground

ADULTS
Lead safety strategy
Account for students and adults

© Copyright 2009–2020, All Rights Reserved. The "I Love U Guys" Foundation, Conifer, CO. The Standard Response Protocol and Logo are Trademarks of The "I Love U Guys" Foundation and may be registered in certain jurisdictions. This material may be duplicated for distribution per "SRP Terms of Use". SRP K12 2021 Poster_EN | v 4.0 | Revised: 04/16/2020 | http://iloveuguys.org

K12 2021 STANDARD RESPONSE PROTOCOL

Note to Printers

This material may be duplicated for distribution per "SRP Terms of Use," which read as follows:

Terms of Use: District/school is responsible for physical material production of any online resources provided by The Foundation. The District/school is not required to utilize printing services provided by The Foundation for production of support materials.

What this means: You may print this material for them.

Terms of Use: School District agrees to incorporate the SRP using the terms of art and the associated directives as defined in the Program Description.

What this means: The school, district, agency or organization may place their logo and/or name on printed material to personalize it. They may not substantively change the wording or actions, except as it applies to hazards specific to their region.

PRINTING THE BOOKS

Books have been laid out with a 5 pica (.83") interior margin and a 4 pica (.63") exterior margin to facilitate duplex printing of the materials. Books can be finished using common bindery methods: perfect bind, comb bind, spiral bind, saddle stitch, or punch for a 3-ring binder.

STATUS POSTERS

Letter-size posters for use to communicate the status of the school during drills or incidents.

These include posters for two levels of Secure conditions, and a Lockdown Drill Poster.

DRILL IN PROGRESS
NO ONE IN OR OUT

SIMULACRO EN CURSO
NO SE PERMITE LA ENTRADA
O SALIDA DE NADIE

SCHOOL IS SECURED
NO ONE IN OR OUT

ESCUELA BAJO PROTECCIÓN
NADIE PUEDE ENTRAR

SCHOOL IS SECURED
MONITORED ENTRY AND CONTROLLED RELEASE

ESCUELA BAJO PROTECCIÓN
ENTRADA VIGILADA Y SALIDA CONTROLADA

PUBLIC ADDRESS PROTOCOL POSTER

The Public Address Protocol Poster can be placed near all reasonable public address locations. This is a sample. Your district, department or agency should customize this poster for regional hazards. It is available to download in Microsoft Word format. The public address is repeated twice each time the public address is performed.

- Hold! In your room or area. Clear the halls.
- Secure! Get Inside. Lock outside doors.
- Lockdown! Locks, Lights, Out of Sight.
- Evacuate! To a Location.
- Shelter! State the Hazard and Safety Strategy.

PARENT HANDOUT
INFORMATION FOR PARENTS AND GUARDIANS

Clear communication to parents and guardians about the SRP is essential so they understand the actions your school will be using. By being as clear as possible, you can reduce the amount of stress they might experience for even the small disruptions in a school day.

They need to understand their roles in any incident. The letter-size handout describes what is expected of people in the school. The other side of the handout, shown here, is Parent Guidance which outlines the roles of the parents and guardians during Secure and Lockdown events.

Schools should outline the methods with which they will be communicating with parents and guardians about any drill or actual incident. It is imperative that parents and guardians keep their contact information up to date with the school and district.

Additionally, there is a web page for parents to go to for detailed information and conversations. Your school or district is welcome to post this on your website for easy access.

The Parent Handout is available in English and Spanish.

IN AN EMERGENCY
TAKE ACTION

HOLD   **SECURE**   **LOCKDOWN**   **EVACUATE**   **SHELTER**

Standard Response Protocol – Public Address	
Medical Emergency	Hold in your Room or Area. Clear the halls.
Threat Outside	Secure! Get inside. Lock outside doors.
Threat Inside	Lockdown! Locks, Lights, Out of Sight!
Bomb	Evacuate to (location) Shelter for Bomb!
Earthquake	Shelter for Earthquake!
Fire Inside	Evacuate to the (location)
Hazmat	Shelter for Hazmat! Seal your Rooms
Weapon	Lockdown! Locks, Lights, Out of Sight!
Tornado	Evacuate to (location) Shelter for Tornado!

STANDARD RESPONSE PROTOCOL

STANDARD RESPONSE PROTOCOL

PARENT GUIDANCE
In the event of a live incident, parents may have questions about their role.

SECURE
"Get Inside. Lock outside doors"

 Secure is called when there is something dangerous outside of the building. Students and staff are brought into the building and the outside doors will be locked. The school might display the Building is Secured poster on entry doors or nearby windows. Inside, it will be business as usual.

SHOULD PARENTS COME TO THE SCHOOL DURING A SECURE EVENT?
Probably not. Every effort is made to conduct classes as normal during a secure event. Additionally, parents may be asked to stay outside during a Secure event.

WHAT IF PARENTS NEED TO PICK UP THEIR STUDENT?
Depending on the situation, it may not be safe to release the student. As the situation evolves, Secure might change to a Monitored Entry and/or Controlled Release.

WILL PARENTS BE NOTIFIED WHEN A SCHOOL GOES INTO SECURE?
When a secure event is brief or the hazard is non-violent, like a wild animal on the playground, there may not be a need to notify parents while the Secure is in place.
With longer or more dangerous events, the school should notify parents that the school has increased their security.

LOCKDOWN
"Locks, Lights, Out of Sight"

 A Lockdown is called when there is something dangerous inside of the building. Students and staff are trained to enter or remain in a room that can be locked, and maintain silence.
A Lockdown is only initiated when there is an active threat inside or very close to the building.

SCHOOL IS SECURE NO ONE IN OR OUT

LA ESCUELA ES SEGURA NADIE PUEDE ENTRAR

SHOULD PARENTS COME TO THE SCHOOL DURING A LOCKDOWN?
The natural inclination for parents is to go to the school during a Lockdown. Understandable, but perhaps problematic. If there is a threat inside the building, law enforcement will be responding. It is unlikely that parents will be granted access to the building or even the campus. If parents are already in the school, they will be instructed to Lockdown as well.

SHOULD PARENTS TEXT THEIR STUDENTS?
The school recognizes the importance of communication between parents and students during a Lockdown event. Parents should be aware though, during the initial period of a Lockdown, it may not be safe for students to text their parents. As the situation resolves, students may be asked to update their parents on a regular basis.
In some cases, students may be evacuated and transported off-site for a student-parent reunification.

WHAT ABOUT UNANNOUNCED DRILLS?
The school may conduct unscheduled drills, however it is highly discouraged to conduct one without announcing that it as a drill. That's called an unannounced drill and can cause undue concern and stress.

Parents should recognize that the school will always inform students that it is a drill during the initial announcement.

It's important to differentiate between a **drill** and an exercise. A drill is used to create the "Muscle Memory" associated with a practiced action. There is no simulation of an event, simply performing the action. An exercise simulates an actual event to test the capacity of personnel and equipment.

DRILL IN PROGRESS NO ONE IN OR OUT

SIMULACRO EN CURSO NO SE PERMITE LA ENTRADA O SALIDA DE NADIE

CAN PARENTS OBSERVE OR PARTICIPATE IN THE DRILLS?
The school welcomes parents who wish to observe or participate in drills.

K12 2021 STANDARD RESPONSE PROTOCOL

RED CARD/GREEN CARD

This is for use in an Evacuation Assembly to do a quick assessment of the status of all groups. It is not for classroom use during a Lockdown or Lockdown Drill.

There are three different types for different situations, so choose to use the one that's best for your environment.

After arriving at an Evacuation Assembly and taking roll, the Red/Green Cards are used for administration or first responders to quickly, visually identify the status of the teachers' classes after an evacuation.

- Green Card (OK) - All students accounted for, No immediate help is necessary
- Red Card (Help) - Extra or missing students, or vital information must be exchanged

RED/GREEN/MED CARD

- Red and White Cross (Medical Help) - Immediate medical attention is needed

RED/GREEN/ROLL CARD

- This includes a roll sheet for users to record who is in their group.

RED/GREEN/ALERT CARD

- The Alert card is used to indicate there is a problem in your group and you need assistance.

VIDEO TRAINING

There are also some videos you can download from http://iloveuguys.org, or YouTube, to use for training purposes.

- **The Standard Response Protocol (SRP) for Students (7:26)**
  This is a teenage student speaking with a School Resource Officer about the actions of the SRP. It's appropriate for students in middle school and older.

- **Lockdown Drill with Standard Response Protocol (3:35)**
  This was recorded during a High School Lockdown drill. It includes interviews with students, and is appropriate for all ages of students.

- **For the very little ones,**
  There are links on the website to training modules that were created for younger students by school districts. We link to those with permission by the creators.

ID CARDS

Art for printing onto identification cards is available for slotted and unslotted cards in the standard size of 3.375" x 2.125".

STANDARD RESPONSE PROTOCOL

HOLD
In your room or area. Clear the halls.

SECURE
Get inside. Lock outside doors.

LOCKDOWN
Locks, lights, out of sight

EVACUATE
To the announced location

SHELTER
Using the announced hazard and strategy

POCKET GUIDE

This is a quick guide to the five actions which folds to the size of a business card to fit in wallets, pockets, and ID card holders. It prints on two sides of a letter-size paper and there are three to a page.

DRILLS vs. Exercises

DRILLS vs. EXERCISES

Media coverage in 2019 exploring issues with lockdown drills potentially causing trauma has resulted in the need for clarification. Much of the coverage attributed the word "Drill" to what was actually an "Exercise."

School lockdown drills, active shooter drills, and exercises are not synonymous. Nor are they universally defined, understood and practiced. Some of this confusion may be a result of actual FEMA guidance (reproduced to the right), and other publicly available materials on the subject.

DRILL

The primary objective of a drill is for participants to build muscle memory, and practice an action to use in various events or situations. A secondary objective is for the people who are administering the drill to validate procedures, clarify roles and identify operational process gaps.

In the school safety context, it is critical to distinguish between drills and exercises. Drills are for staff and students, and are educational opportunities to practice a life safety skill.

EXERCISE

The over-all learning objective of an exercise is to test response, capacity and resources across the system. An exercise often includes a description or enactment of an incident, depending on the type of exercise that's being conducted.

Exercises are broader in scope. These typically present a hypothetical emergency scenario (hurricane, earthquake, biochemical emergency, etc.) designed to encourage people to think on their toes, work together, and apply lessons learned from drills.

Invite people from your community to participate as volunteers in an Exercise, or to observe it. You will probably be introducing scenarios they have thought about; this level of engagement can be quite useful.

A **Tabletop Exercise** is a roundtable session administered by a facilitator. Team members discuss their roles and share observations regarding a simulated emergency scenario. It's designed to test each member's ability to refer and react to their role in the emergency plan, as well as their readiness to communicate with other members as needed. These usually run a few hours in duration, and are highly valuable for identifying the unique threats in each community.

In a **Functional Exercise**, participants perform their duties in a simulated emergency environment. Functional exercises typically focus on specific team members and/or procedures, and are often used to identify process gaps associated with multi-agency coordination, command and control.

A **Full-Scale Exercise** is similar in execution to a functional exercise, and is as close to the real thing as possible. It can include employees from multiple functions, community first responders, local businesses, and regulatory agencies. This type of exercise should utilize, to the extent possible, the actual systems and equipment that would be dispatched during a real event. From a duration standpoint, full-scale exercises often take place over the course of an entire business day.

SRP EVOLUTION

In developing the Standard Response Protocol, The "I Love U Guys" Foundation took the following approach:

- Identify the hazard;
- Develop response;
- Train;
- Practice;
- Drill;
- Exercise.

DRILL IN PROGRESS NO ONE IN OR OUT

SIMULACRO EN CURSO NO SE PERMITE LA ENTRADA O SALIDA DE NADIE

K12 2021 STANDARD RESPONSE PROTOCOL

PROBLEM IDENTIFICATION

The first priority of the SRP was to introduce common, plain language responses to various events. Assessment of various school responses in 2009 revealed there was no common language between students, staff, parents, media and first responders. The core areas examined were:

- Something happening outside the school;
- Something happening inside of the school;
- How to get out of the school;
- Natural or man-made hazards;
- Keeping the halls clear.

DEVELOP RESPONSE

Given those conditions, the Standard Response Protocol was developed, piloted and released.

TRAIN

The next step in the process is providing training to students and staff on each of the response protocols. For example, the Foundation has developed materials for training students and staff on the SRP.

PRACTICE

Once training has been delivered, practice is recommended prior to any drill. This may initially involve a discussion between staff and students to:

- Find various exit routes in advance of an Evacuation drill;
- Discuss ways to protect oneself from various weather hazards prior to a Shelter drill;
- Identify Safe Zones within a classroom and practice moving students to those zones prior to a Lockdown drill;
- Talk about situations that may require a Secure or Hold action.

COMMUNICATING ABOUT DRILLS

Prior to conducting any drills, schools are advised to send concise communication to parents and guardians about the nature and objectives of, and reason for, the drill. This can be done with an email or letter or both. It is not necessary to state the exact day or time of the certain drills.

If parents feel thier student(s) will be upset by certain drills, invite them to attend the drill, or give them a chance to opt their family out of the drill. If possible, arrange to have an opt-out student stay on school grounds, but not participate, in order to minimize disruption to the school day.

FEMA GUIDANCE - IS-362.A

FEMA guidance on training, drilling and exercising, from the course IS-362.A *"Multihazard Emergency Planning for Schools."*

"

TRAINING

- **Briefings:** Short meetings that provide information about a specific topic (e.g., new evacuation sites, tips on how to use the student information system to find student contact information, new district contact information).
- **Seminars/classroom training:** Used to introduce new programs, policies, or procedures. Provide information to students and staff on roles and responsibilities. This may also include training presented outside of the school (e.g., first aid, CERT).
- **Workshops:** Resemble a seminar but are employed to build specific products, such as a draft plan or policy.

DRILLS

Drills are operations-based exercises that usually test a single specific operation or function within a single entity. Conducted in a realistic environment, drills are often used to test new policies or equipment, practice current skills, or prepare for larger scale exercises.

FUNCTIONAL EXERCISE

A functional exercise is the simulation of an emergency event that:

- Involves various levels of school, school district, and emergency management personnel.
- Involves trained personnel "acting out" their actual roles.
- Evaluates both the internal capabilities and responses of the school, school district, and emergency management officials.
- Evaluates the coordination activities between the school, school district, and emergency management personnel.

FULL-SCALE EXERCISE

- A full-scale exercise is a multiagency, multijurisdictional, multidiscipline operations-based exercise involving functional (e.g., Joint Field Office, emergency operations center) and "boots on the ground" response (e.g., firefighters decontaminating mock victims). "

https://emilms.fema.gov/IS362a/ (Circa 2019.06.12)

LOCKDOWN Drills

LOCKDOWN DRILL GUIDANCE

A critical aspect in implementing the SRP with fidelity is the Lockdown Drill. Successful drills provide participants with the "muscle memory" should an actual Lockdown occur. Drills also reveal deficiencies that may exist in either procedures, training or personnel.

Understand that a lockdown drill is for practicing an action, not an event. An actual lockdown can occur due to a variety of threatening situations which may present an immediate and ongoing danger to the safety of students, staff and visitors within a building.

PREPARATION

Prior to drilling, students, staff and administration should review the SRP Training Presentation, which is available on The "I Love U Guys" Foundation website. Administration should also verify with law enforcement their use of the SRP in the school or district.

Teachers should take time with students to identify and occupy a "Safe Zone" in the classroom where they cannot be seen through any corridor windows. If visibility in a classroom is problematic, window coverings or alternative locations should be identified. Speak with local law enforcement about their preference about using window coverings.

Additionally, the following instructions should be delivered to students.

1. Locate yourself at a point in the classroom where you can no longer see out the corridor window.
2. Maintain silence. No cell phone calls.
3. Refrain from texting during drills.

PARTNERSHIPS

School level drills should have district support. There may also be district resources available to assist in conducting the drill. Another key partnership is with local law enforcement. Local patrol, community resource officers or school resource officers should be part of the drill process.

THE EMERGENCY RESPONSE TEAM

Some schools have a pre-identified Building/School Emergency Response Team. These teams are effective for responding to any type of incident.

It is a noted best practice for administration to survey the staff population for prior emergency response, military or law enforcement experience, specialized training and skills for use in district emergency operations.

THE LOCKDOWN DRILL TEAM

During an actual lockdown, members of the Emergency Response Team may be in classrooms or administrative offices in lockdown mode and unable to assist with the response.

The Lockdown Drill Team should not include personnel that have specific roles during an actual emergency within that school. Instead, the team might include a school nurse or medical professional, district safety representatives, law enforcement, and those administrators from another school.

STAFF NOTIFICATION

When lockdown drills are first being introduced to a school, it is absolutely okay to tell staff in advance of the drill. There may be staff members adversely affected by surprise drills.

SPECIAL NEEDS CONSIDERATIONS

It is critical to identify any specific issues that may cause challenges for students with special needs or disabilities and incorporate appropriate actions for notification prior to drills. It is not recommended that additional assistance be provided in special needs areas for drills, UNLESS this assistance is part of the plan and those resources will be assigned in an actual emergency.

THE PRE-DRILL BRIEFING

Prior to the lockdown drill a short planning meeting with the Lockdown Drill Team should occur. The agenda is simple:

1. Review the floor plan and team member assignments;
2. Expected drill duration;
3. The door knock and classroom conversation;
4. Potential student or staff distress.

OPTIONS-BASED TRAINING

Both staff and students should be educated about the options that can be used in an active threat situation. Realistically, students and staff are not always in their classrooms or behind closed doors as they go throughout their busy school days; because of this, students and staff should be taught additional strategies that go beyond Locking Down in a classroom. Possible discussion can include what a staff member or student should do when in a bathroom, cafeteria, or hallway if an active threat arises. This is where self-evacuation strategies could play a roll.

Lockdown drills can be conducted at varied times, such as when some classes are outside or at recess. The staff and students at recess can practice how to safely leave the school grounds Age-appropriate strategies can be discussed.

ANNOUNCING THE LOCKDOWN DRILL

When using public address to announce a lockdown drill, repeat, "Lockdown. Locks, Lights, Out of Sight. This is a drill." It's important to tell students and staff that this is a drill. Failure to do so will most likely result in parents, media and maybe even law enforcement coming to the school.

"Lockdown. Locks, Lights, Out of Sight. This is a drill. Lockdown. Locks, Lights, Out of Sight. This is a drill."

Alternately, consider announcing the drill prior to saying which type of drill it is. This technique will prevent an immediate reaction to the word Lockdown.

"This is a drill. Lockdown. Locks, Lights, Out of Sight"
"This is a drill. Lockdown. Locks, Lights, Out of Sight,"

or

"We are going to conduct a lockdown drill. Please listen for the lockdown announcement."

CONDUCTING THE DRILL

The Lockdown Drill Team should be broken into groups of two or three members who go to individual classrooms. One of the members acts as "Scribe" and documents each classroom response. Large schools will need multiple Lockdown Drill Teams in order to complete the drill in a timely fashion.

At the classroom door, team members listen for noise and look through the corridor window for any student or staff visibility or movement. A team member then knocks on the door and requests entry. There should be no response to this request. At this point a member of the team unlocks the classroom door and announces their name and position. A quick assessment is made by the safety team. The occupants of the room are reminded that they are still in lockdown and should remain so until they hear an announcement that the drill is completed.

A Lockdown Response Worksheet was created by The "I Love U Guys" Foundation to assist you in conducting and documenting your lockdown drills. See Appendix A.

WINDOWS

Often there is a conversation about inside and outside windows. Corridor windows are left uncovered so that first responders can see inside the room. Outside windows are left untouched because the threat would be inside the building. There are different preferences regarding window coverings, so please discuss this with your local responders to make sure you're in agreement.

THE CLASSROOM CONVERSATION

Make sure to stake out a few minutes after the room has been checked, and before the release of the drill, to allow for conversation in the classroom.

Typically, this conversation addresses the purpose of the drill, and the observed outcome for that classroom. Additionally, self-evacuation and other life safety strategies can be discussed.

Any issues should be addressed gently but immediately. When possible, have a school counselor available to address any staff or student distress.

THE LOCKDOWN DRILL TEAM DEBRIEF

At the conclusion of the drill, the team should reconvene for a debrief, and use this time to review portions of the school safety plan. A good debriefing may reveal some gaps and areas for improvement in the plan.

Any issues should be documented, and action items identified. An opportunity for all staff to submit information regarding the performance of the drill should be part of the after action review process.

LOCKDOWN DRILLS OR ACTIVE SHOOTER DRILLS?

A Lockdown Drill is designed to practice for any threat inside the building and to create the muscle memory. Therefore these Drills should only be for Lockdown, and not "active shooter "or "active assailant."

One of the primary goals of crisis preparedness is to develop a sense of empowerment and control. Lockdown drills not conducted appropriately may cause physical and psychological harm to students, staff, and the overall learning environment. An active shooter or armed assailant **exercise** is specific to one type of incident, with the intended outcome of first responders and schools practicing their tactics. These include simulating a hazardous event, in which case it is more accurate to define them as **Exercises**.

When these are conducted, participants (staff and students) must willingly volunteer, and understand exactly what the scenario will be.

STANDARD RESPONSE PROTOCOL

FREQUENTLY ASKED QUESTIONS

Since introducing the Standard Response Protocol in 2009, thousands of districts, departments and agencies have scrutinized, evaluated and ultimately implemented the program. During the process some questions seem to come up often.

SERIOUSLY, WHAT DOES IT REALLY COST?

Since its introduction in 2009, public K12 schools, districts, departments and agencies were free to use The "I Love U Guys" Foundation programs at no cost.

In 2015, the Foundation expanded availability, and now offers the programs to any public or private organization at no charge. Download the materials and begin the process.

WHAT ABOUT BUSINESS/CHURCH/ INSTITUTION USE?

Please look at the materials designed specifically for institutional use on the website. http://iloveuguys.org.

I SEE YOU OFFER TRAINING. DO WE NEED TO BUY TRAINING IN ORDER TO USE THE PROGRAMS?

No. We've attempted to put enough material online so that schools and law enforcement can successfully implement Foundation programs. We know of thousands of schools across the US and Canada that have implemented the programs using internal resources.

That said, part of our sustainability model relies not just on charitable giving, but in providing training for districts departments and agencies. If your organization is interested in Foundation training, please contact us for rates and terms.

WHAT IS THE DIFFERENCE BETWEEN SECURE AND LOCKDOWN AGAIN?

The term "Secure" is used when there is a potential threat that can be mitigated by bringing everyone inside. It should be announced with the directive "Get inside. Lock outside doors," which signals to bring people in and lock exterior doors. While it calls for heightened situational awareness, it also allows for indoor activities to continue.

The term "Lockdown" means there is an active or imminent threat inside or nearby requiring immediate protective action. It is followed by the directive "Locks, Lights, Out of Sight" and requires locking classroom doors, turning out the lights, and remaining hidden until first responders arrive.

Effectively if the threat is outside the building, Secure. If the threat is inside the building, Lockdown.

WHAT IF THE THREAT IS CLOSE TO THE BUILDING?

There may be situations where both Secure and Lockdown protocols may be called sequentially. In this case, use Secure to get people inside and lock exterior doors. When the perimeter is Secured, this may become a Lockdown if the threat is persistent and appears to be coming closer. Exterior doors would stay locked.

IN LOCKDOWN, YOU SUGGEST UNLOCKING THE OUTSIDE DOORS. WHAT'S UP WITH THAT?

No, we don't. We occasionally hear this but our guidance is actually a little different. We suggest not putting anyone at risk by locking or unlocking outside doors. If the doors are locked, leave them locked. Be sure you have a plan in advance that allows first responders the ability to enter the building quickly.

WON'T PEOPLE STILL COME IN THE BUILDING IF THE OUTSIDE DOORS ARE UNLOCKED DURING A LOCKDOWN?

Yes, people may be able to enter the building during the window of time between calling a lockdown and the arrival of first responders.

A lockdown is called when there is a life safety threat inside the building. During the development and throughout the lifecycle of the SRP, constant and deliberate scrutiny of all risk/benefit guidance is performed by the Foundation, district and law enforcement representatives. This has resulted in the lockdown guidance provided.

That said, with any guidance provided, we defer to local decisions. If you are a district, please consult with your local law enforcement representatives for final guidance.

I THOUGHT I SAW SHELTER GUIDANCE?

When we developed the SRP and released the first version in 2009 we included FEMA guidance regarding the Shelter directive and actions. FEMA changed that guidance in 2014. We are removing specific shelter guidance from our documentation and defer to the current practices published at http://fema.gov as well as your local emergency management guidance.

CAN THE SRP BE USED IN CONJUNCTION WITH OTHER SAFETY PLANS?

Yes, absolutely. The SRP is designed as an enhancement to any safety plan. It covers critical incidents by standardizing vocabulary so stakeholders can easily understand the status and respond quickly when an unforeseen event occurs. Comprehensive safety plans will include components such as communications, threat assessment, local hazards, operation continuity and reunification, among other items.

CAN I MODIFY MATERIALS?

That depends. The core actions and directives must remain intact. These are:

1. Hold "In your room or area. Clear the halls."

2. Secure "Get inside. Locks outside doors"

3. Lockdown "Locks, Lights, Out of Sight"

4. Evacuate followed by the announced location

5. Shelter followed by the announced hazard and safety strategy

Some details may need to be customized to your location. For instance, the classroom poster should be modified to include hazards and safety strategies that are specific to your location.

ARE THE SOURCE MATERIALS AVAILABLE?

Yes. Some of the materials are available. Original, digital artwork can be provided to organizations that have signed "Memorandum of Understanding" with The "I Love U Guys" Foundation.

Please note: Currently, original artwork is only provided in Mac OS X, Pages version 10.0 or QuarkXPress 2019 (15.2.1).

CAN YOU SEND ME MATERIALS IN MICROSOFT WORD?

The Public Address Poster, and all MOUs and NOIs are produced in Word. The other materials are not. Retaining the graphic integrity of the materials proved beyond our capabilities using Microsoft Word.

CAN I REALLY USE THE MATERIALS? WHAT ABOUT COPYRIGHTS AND TRADEMARKS?

Schools, districts, departments, agencies and organizations are free to use the materials under the "Terms of Use" outlined in this document and in the Memorandum of Understanding.

DO I NEED TO ASK PERMISSION TO USE THE MATERIALS?

No. You really don't need to ask permission. But, it would be great if you let us know that you're using our programs.

DO I HAVE TO SIGN AN MOU WITH THE FOUNDATION?

It is not necessary to sign an MOU with the Foundation, but please consider it. The Foundation is committed to providing programs at no cost. Yet, program development, enhancement, and support are cost centers for us. One way we fund those costs is through private grants and funding.

An MOU is a strong demonstration of program validity and assists us with these types of funding requests.

When you submit a completed MOU or NOI, you will be added to our database and notified when updates and new materials are available.

DO I HAVE TO SEND A NOTICE OF INTENT?

In the absence of an MOU, a Notice of Intent provides similar value to us regarding demonstrations of program validity to potential funders. Either one means that you will receive notification of updates and new materials.

DO I HAVE TO NOTIFY YOU AT ALL THAT I AM USING THE SRP?

We often speak with school safety stakeholders that have implemented the SRP, but hadn't quite mentioned it to us. Please let us know that your school, district, department or agency is using the SRP.

It is our goal that the SRP becomes the "Gold Standard." The more schools, districts, departments and agencies that we can show are using the program, the greater the chance for achieving our goal of having clear communication in a crisis.

CAN I PUT OUR LOGO ON YOUR MATERIALS?

Yes. But with some caveats. If you are a school, district, department or agency you may include your logo on posters and handouts. If you are a commercial enterprise, please contact us in advance with intended usage.

In some states, we have co-branding agreements with "umbrella" organizations (school district self insurance pools, school safety centers, etc.). In those states, we ask that you also include the umbrella organization's branding.

WE WOULD LIKE TO PUT THE MATERIALS ON OUR WEBSITE.

Communication with your community is important. While you are free to place any material on your website, it's preferable that you link to the materials from our website. The reason for this is to allow us to track material usage. We can then use these numbers when we seek funding.

But, don't let that be a show stopper. If your IT group prefers, just copy the materials to your site.

DOES THE SRP WORK WITH "RUN, HIDE, FIGHT?"

In 2014, the Department of Education suggested "Run, Hide, Fight" as the preferred response to an active shooter. We don't believe the practice is mutually exclusive to the SRP, as that is a single-incident response. Again, consult with local law enforcement regarding your specific active shooter response.

There may be some challenges regarding training students using some of the "Run, Hide, Fight" materials. The Department of Education suggests "These videos are not recommended for viewing by minors."

DOES THE SRP WORK WITH A.L.I.C.E.?

Again, we don't believe that SRP and A.L.I.C.E. (single incident response) are mutually exclusive.

DOES THE SRP WORK WITH "AVOID, DENY, DEFEND?"

The SRP attempts to be an all-hazards approach to school based events. Of all of the active shooter responses, our determination is that "Avoid, Deny, Defend" from Texas State University has the best positioning, linguistics and actions. This response was created for adults and is for use in workplaces.

http://www.avoiddenydefend.org

APPENDIX A - LOCKDOWN DRILL WORKSHEET

The Lockdown Drill Worksheet was created to assist you when conducting Lockdown Drills. The Options check boxes are used when the people in the room chose to perform some optional actions.

LOCKDOWN DRILL
WORKSHEET

School _____

Date/Time _____

Team Members _____

_____

_____

Stopwatch Time _____ Student Population _____ Staff Count _____

Room#							
Locks	□ Yes □ No	□ Yes □ No	□ Yes □ No	□ Yes □ No	□ Yes □ No	□ Yes □ No	□ Yes □ No
Lights	□ Yes □ No	□ Yes □ No	□ Yes □ No	□ Yes □ No	□ Yes □ No	□ Yes □ No	□ Yes □ No
Out of Sight	□ Yes □ No	□ Yes □ No	□ Yes □ No	□ Yes □ No	□ Yes □ No	□ Yes □ No	□ Yes □ No
Door Knock	□ Yes □ No	□ Yes □ No	□ Yes □ No	□ Yes □ No	□ Yes □ No	□ Yes □ No	□ Yes □ No
Why?	□ Yes □ No	□ Yes □ No	□ Yes □ No	□ Yes □ No	□ Yes □ No	□ Yes □ No	□ Yes □ No
Options	□ Yes □ No	□ Yes □ No	□ Yes □ No	□ Yes □ No	□ Yes □ No	□ Yes □ No	□ Yes □ No

Notes _____

_____

_____

_____

Room#							
Locks	□ Yes □ No	□ Yes □ No	□ Yes □ No	□ Yes □ No	□ Yes □ No	□ Yes □ No	□ Yes □ No
Lights	□ Yes □ No	□ Yes □ No	□ Yes □ No	□ Yes □ No	□ Yes □ No	□ Yes □ No	□ Yes □ No
Out of Sight	□ Yes □ No	□ Yes □ No	□ Yes □ No	□ Yes □ No	□ Yes □ No	□ Yes □ No	□ Yes □ No
Door Knock	□ Yes □ No	□ Yes □ No	□ Yes □ No	□ Yes □ No	□ Yes □ No	□ Yes □ No	□ Yes □ No
Why?	□ Yes □ No	□ Yes □ No	□ Yes □ No	□ Yes □ No	□ Yes □ No	□ Yes □ No	□ Yes □ No
Options	□ Yes □ No	□ Yes □ No	□ Yes □ No	□ Yes □ No	□ Yes □ No	□ Yes □ No	□ Yes □ No

Notes _____

_____

_____

_____

Made in the USA
Columbia, SC
18 May 2021